TRADITIONAL IRISH
A Bunch Of Thyme

Allegro

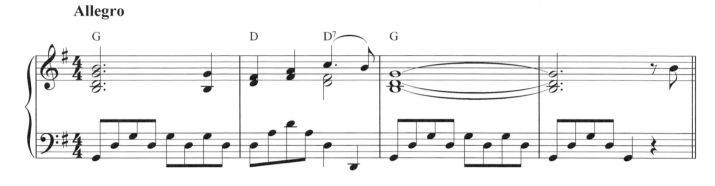

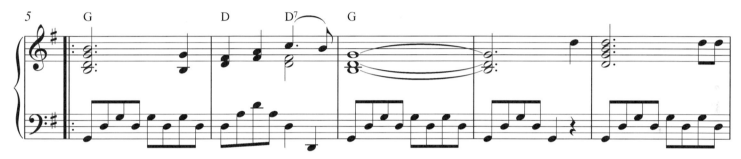

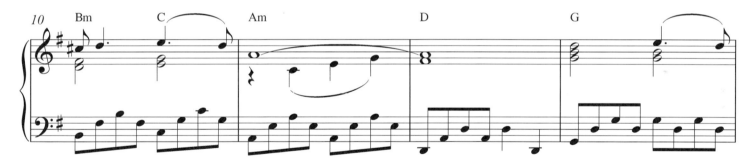

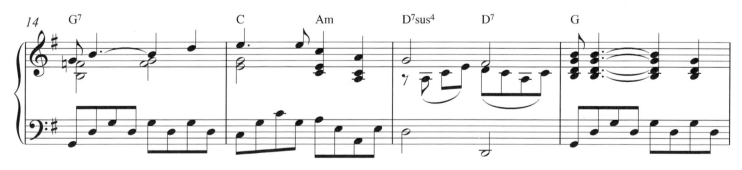

JOHN DENVER
Annie's Song

Words & Music by John Denver

Moderato ♩ = 142

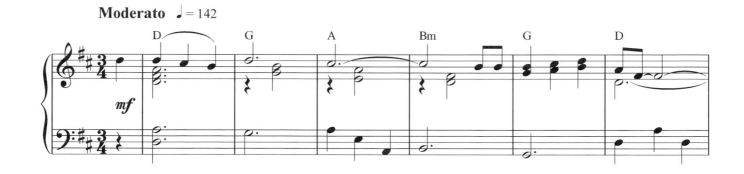

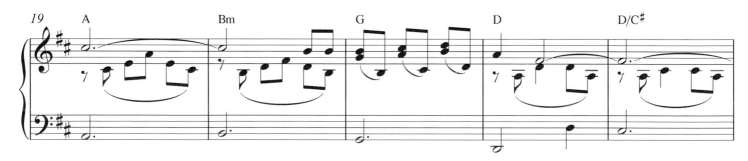

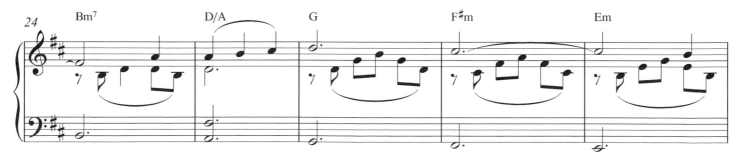

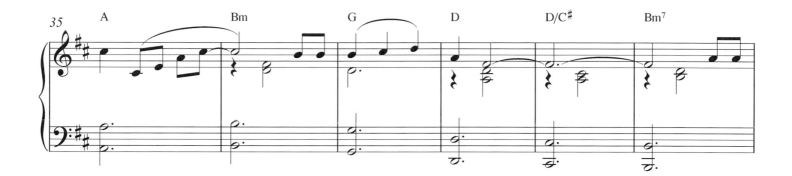

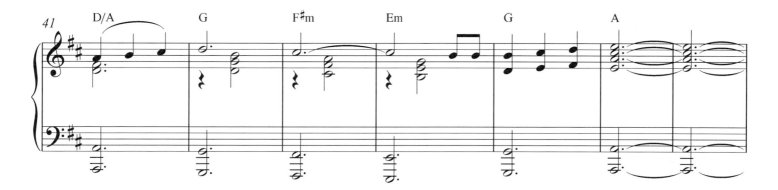

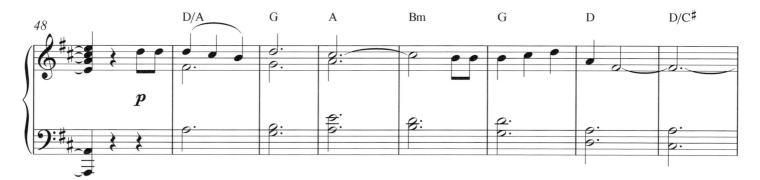

TRADITIONAL IRISH
The Black Velvet Band

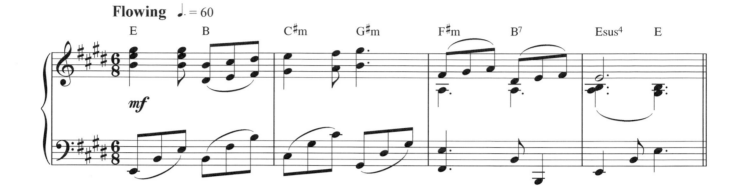

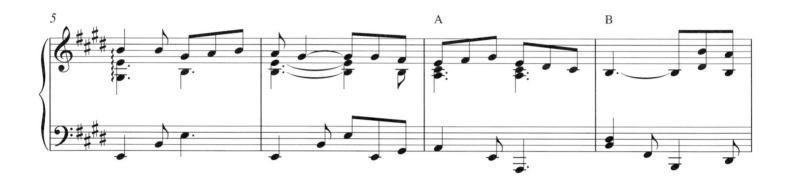

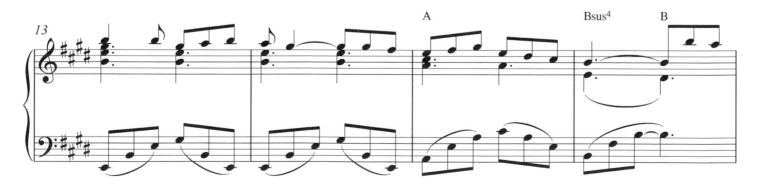

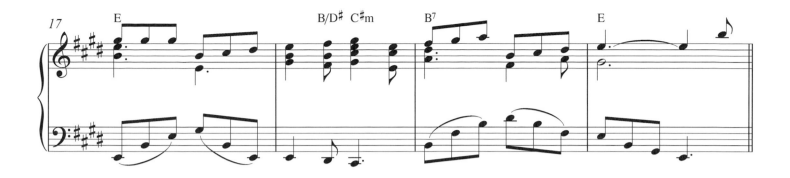

9

THE CORRS
Breathless

Words & Music by R.J. Lange, Andrea Corr, Caroline Corr, Sharon Corr & Jim Corr

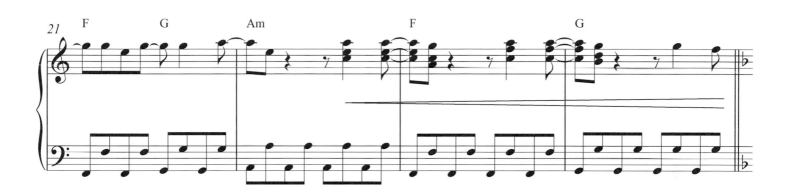

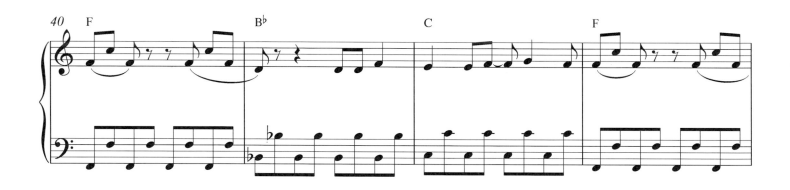

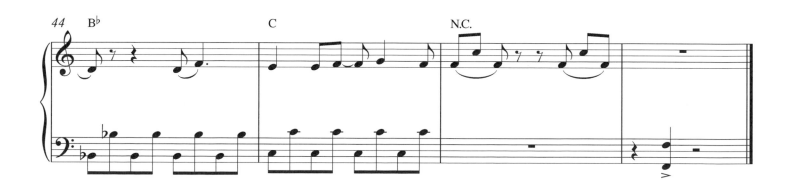

TRADITIONAL IRISH
Carrickfergus

Arranged by Barrie Carson Turner

Relaxed, slow beat ♩ = 58

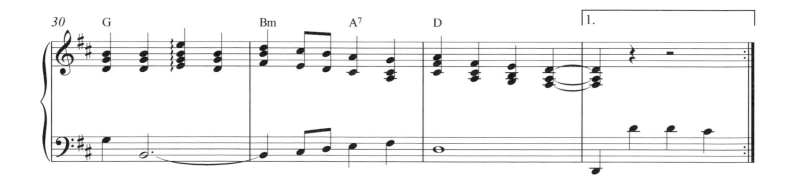

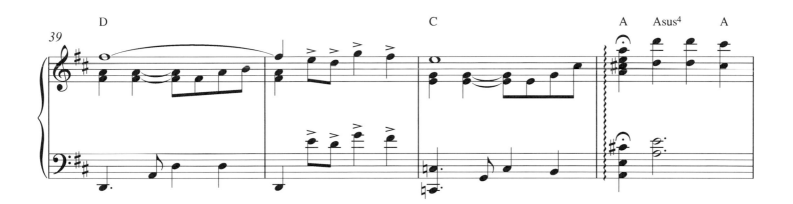

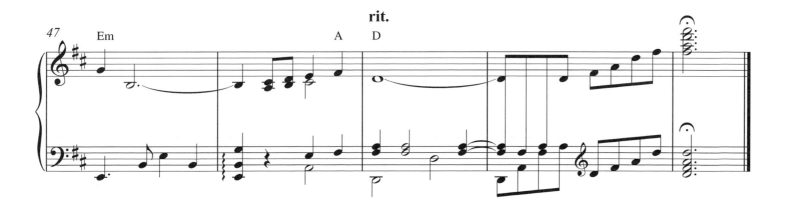

TRADITIONAL IRISH
Cockles and Mussels
(Molly Malone)

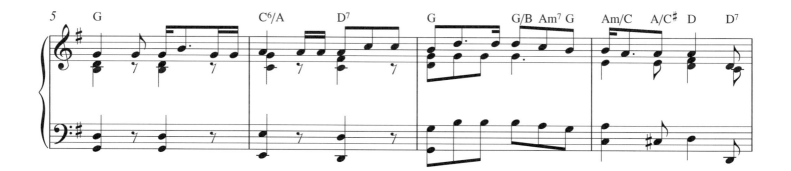

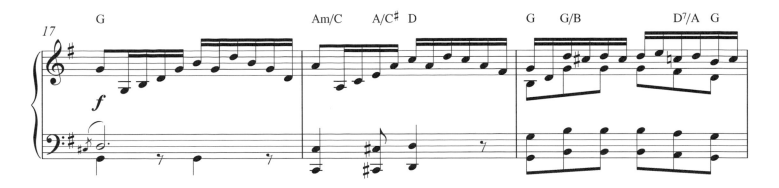

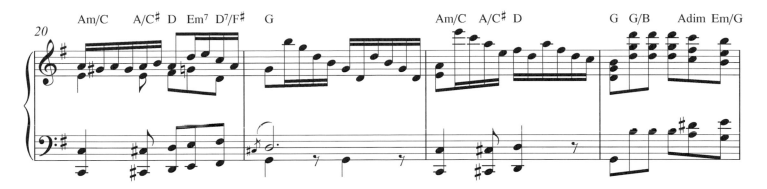

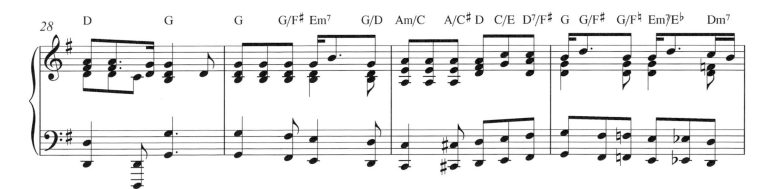

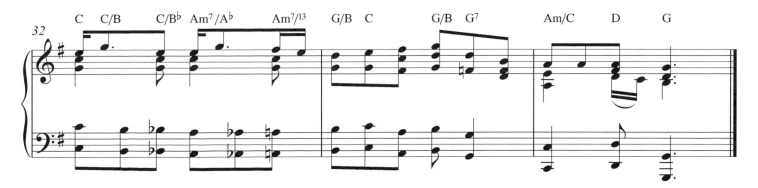

TRADITIONAL IRISH
Drowsy Maggie

Arranged by Matthew King

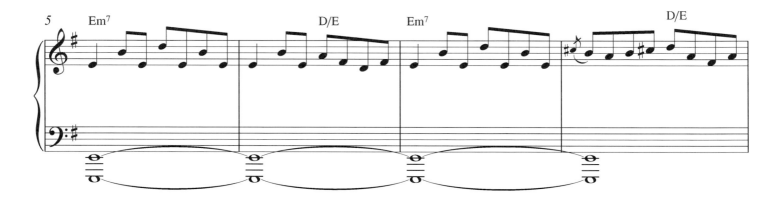

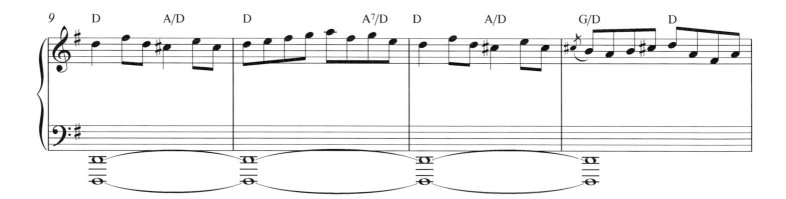

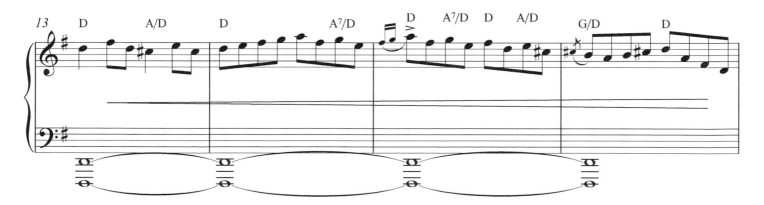

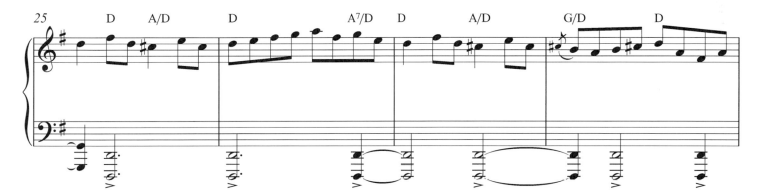

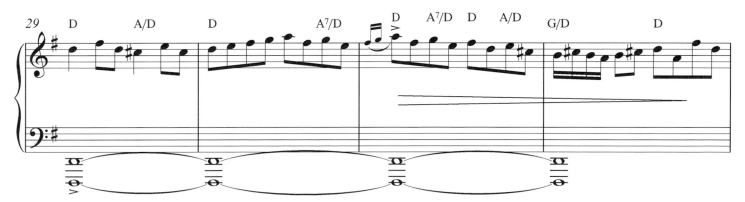

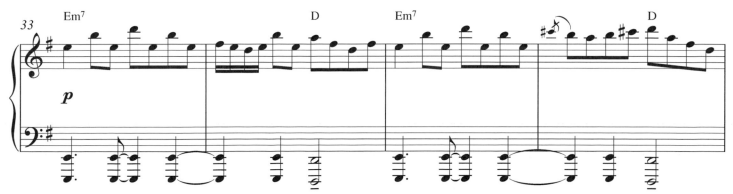

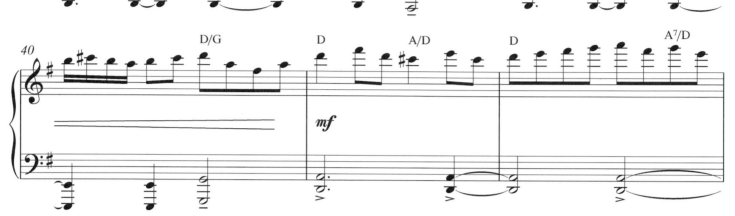

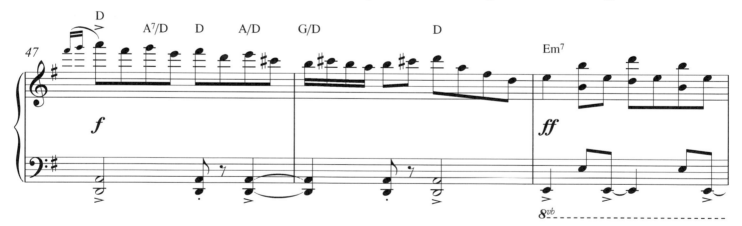

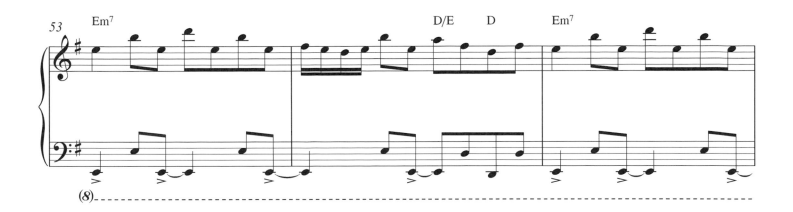

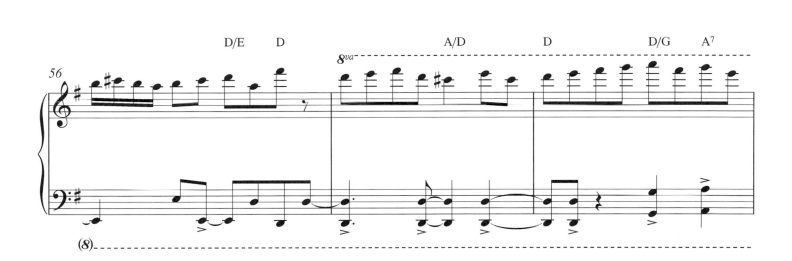

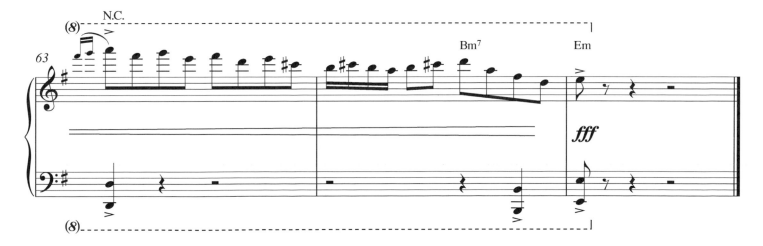

TRADITIONAL IRISH
Eileen Alannah

Words & Music by J.R. Thomas

Fairly slow

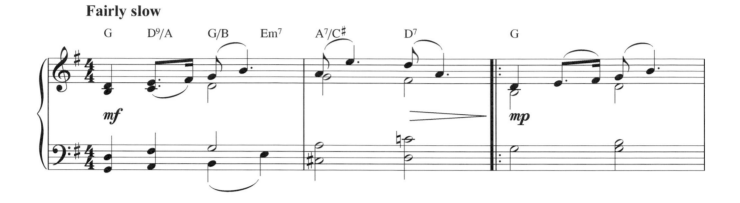

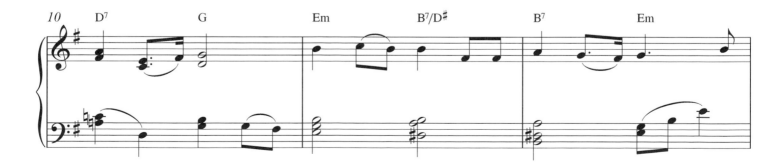

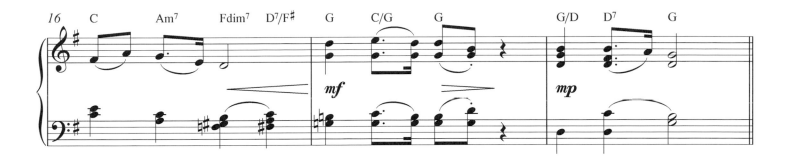

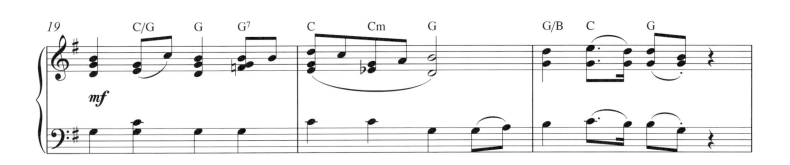

THE POGUES
Fairytale Of New York

Words & Music by Shane MacGowan & Jem Finer

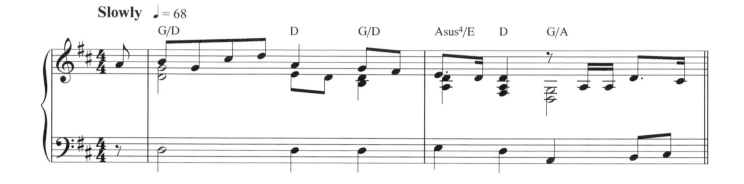

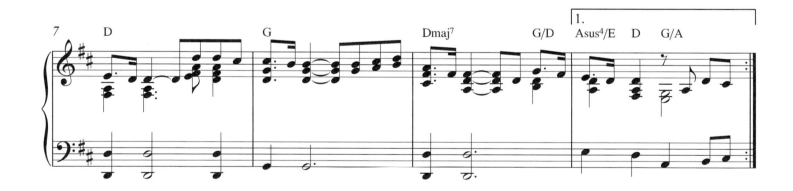

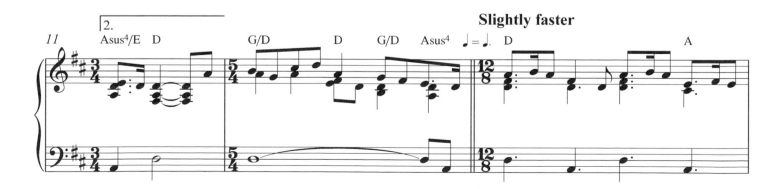

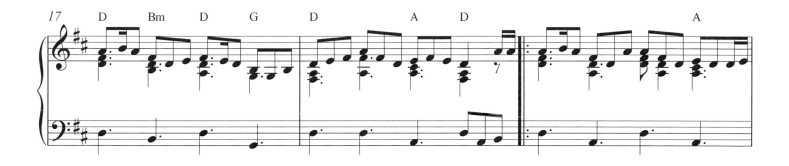

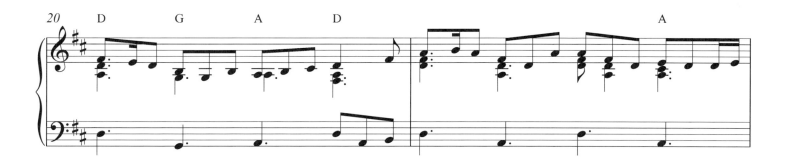

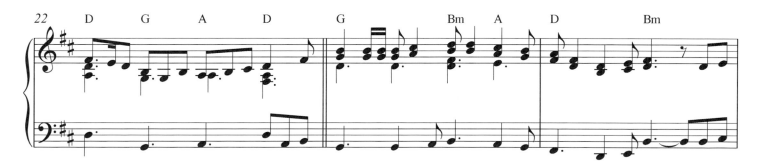

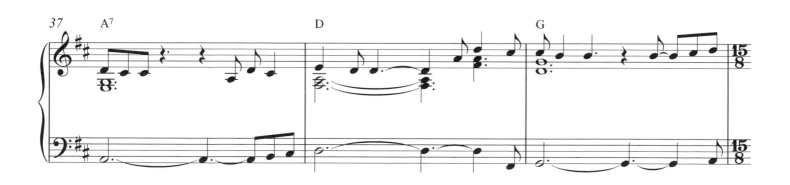

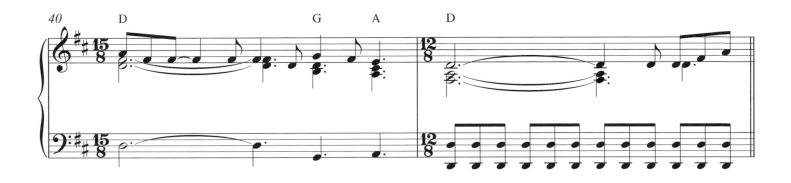

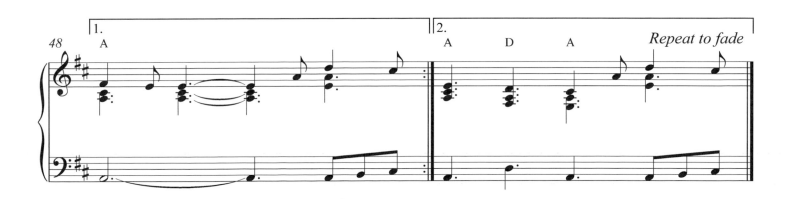

TRADITIONAL IRISH
Finnegan's Wake

Brisk, but not too fast

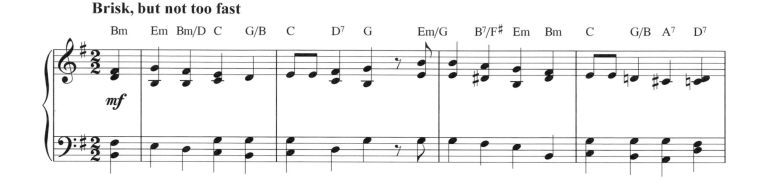

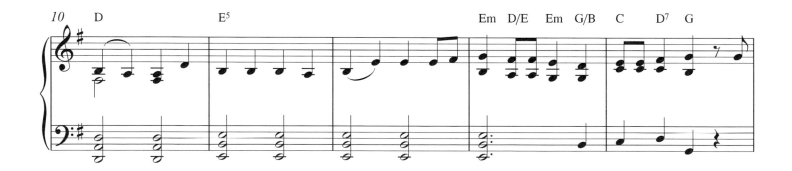

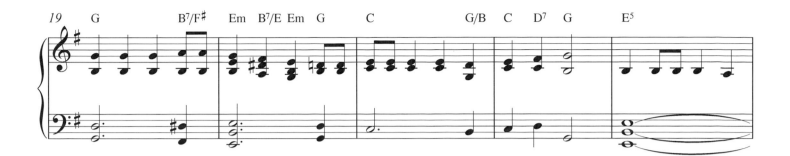

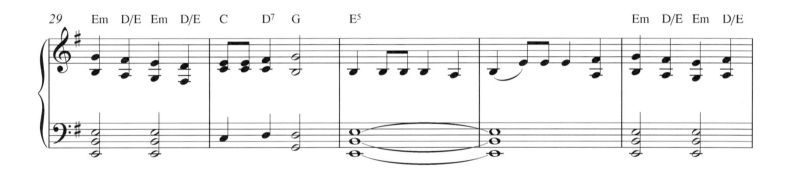

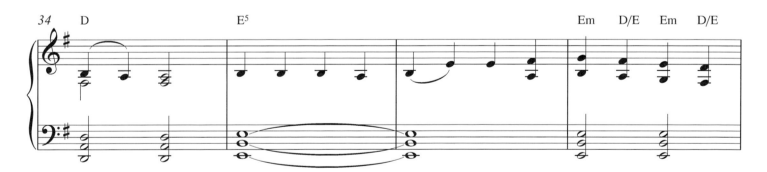

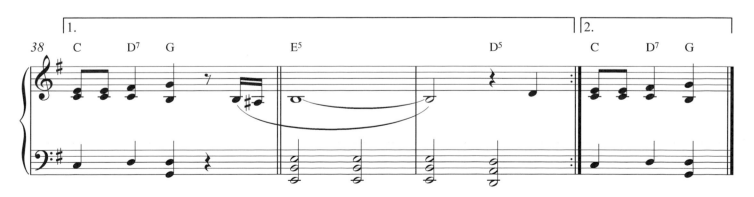

THE CHIEFTAINS
Friel's Kitchen

Traditional, arranged by Sean Keane

This arrangement by Barrie Carson Turner

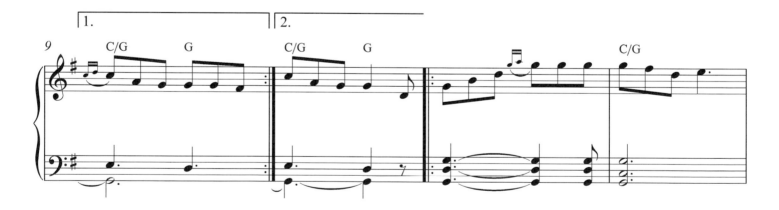

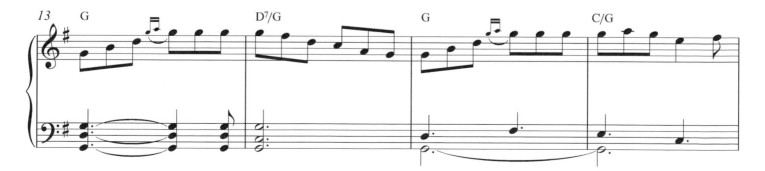

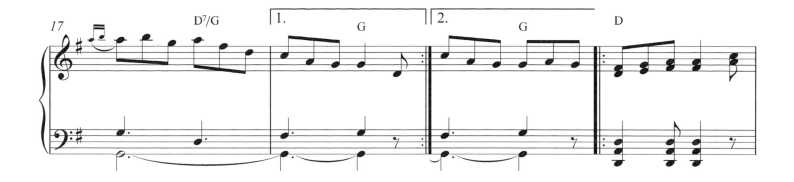

D.S. (with repeats)

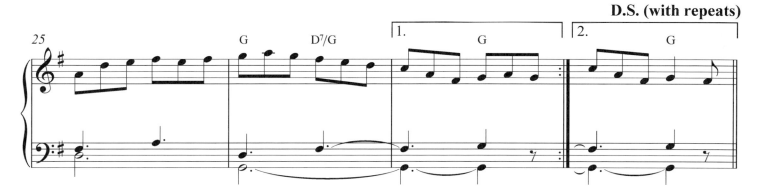

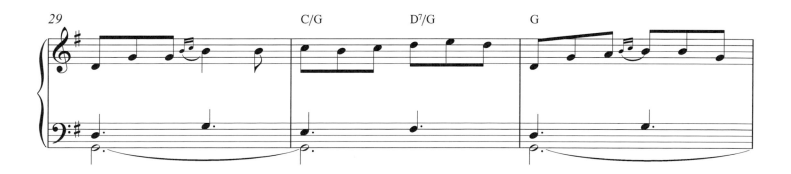

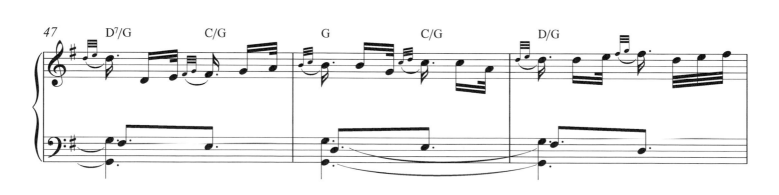

TRADITIONAL IRISH
Danny Boy
(Londonderry Air)

Words by Fred E. Weatherly

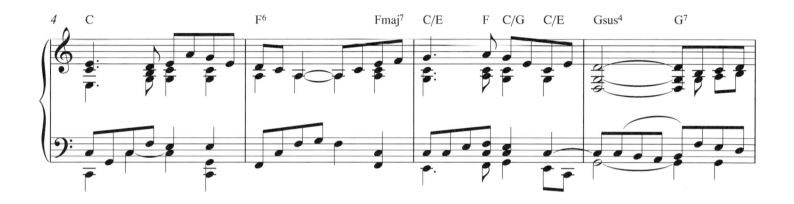

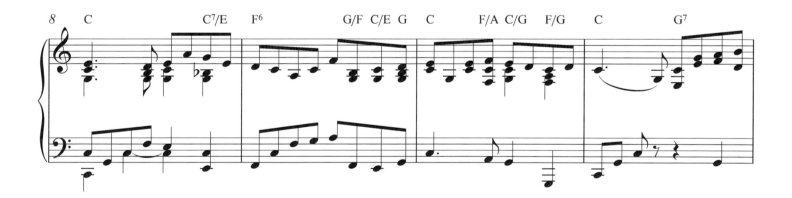

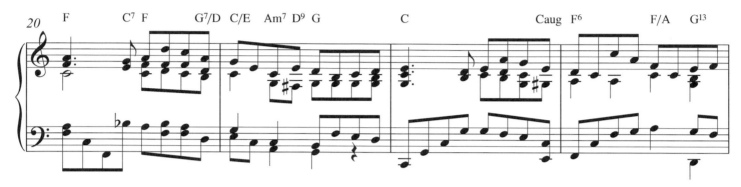

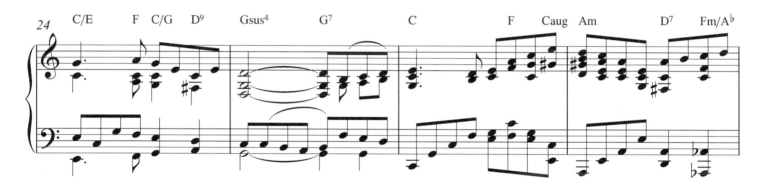

34

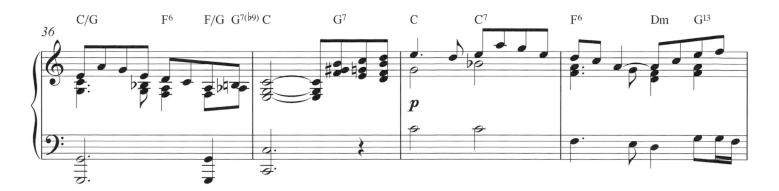

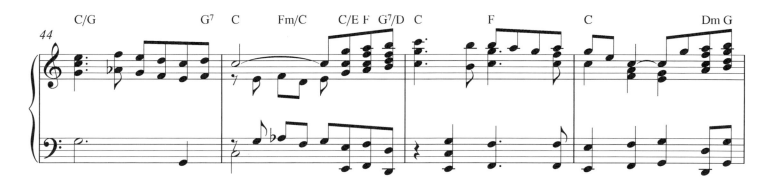

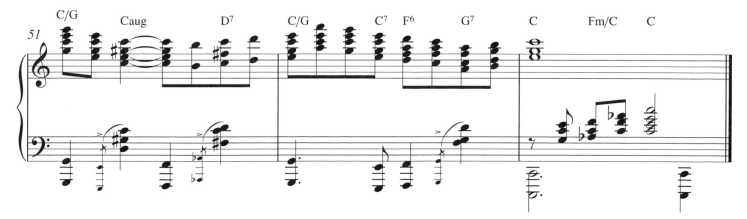

THE BOOMTOWN RATS
I Don't Like Mondays

Words & Music by Bob Geldof

Energetically ♩ = 142

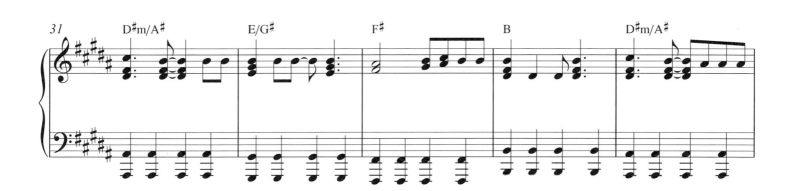

37

TRADITIONAL IRISH
It's A Long Way To Tipperary

Words & Music by Jack Judge & Harry Williams

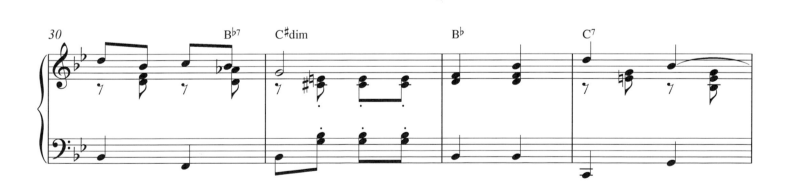

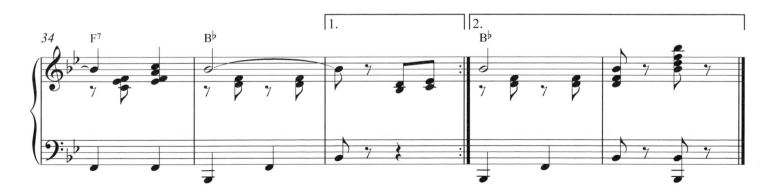

TRADITIONAL IRISH
The Kerry Dance

Music by J. L. Molloy

Bright

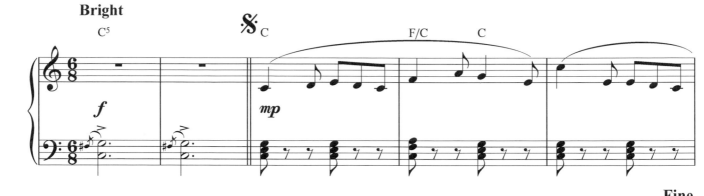

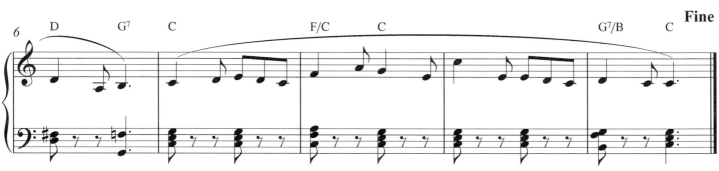

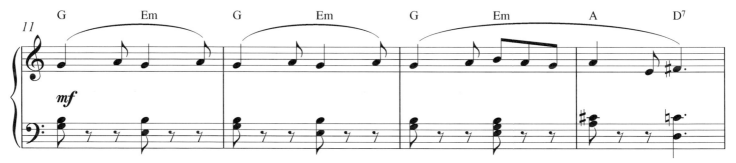

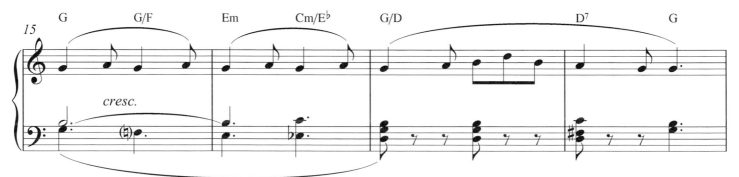

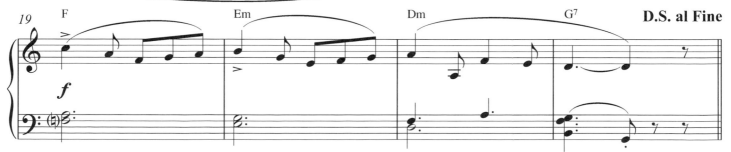

TRADITIONAL IRISH
The Minstrel Boy

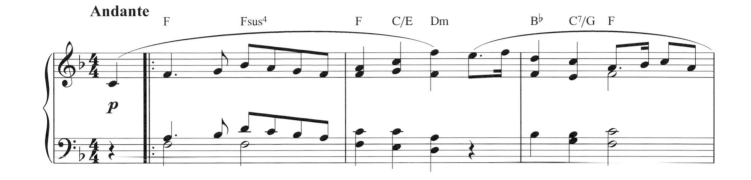

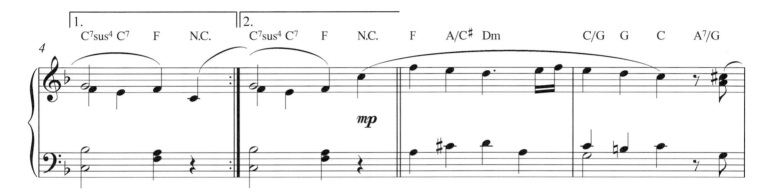

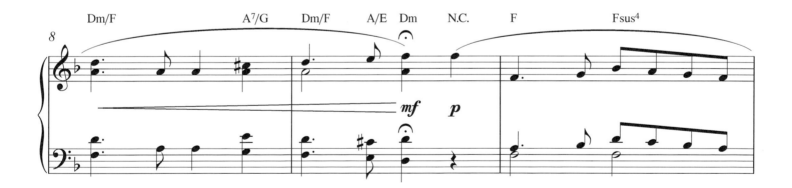

TRADITIONAL IRISH
The Mountains Of Mourne

Words & Music by Percy French & Houston Collisson

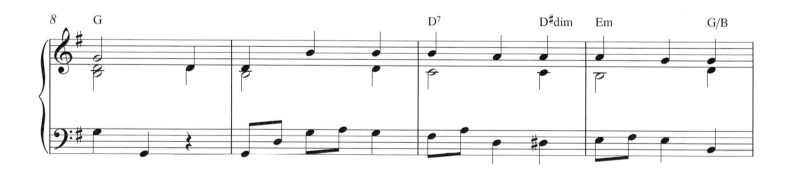

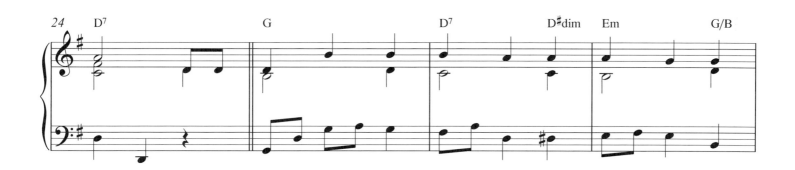

TRADITIONAL IRISH
My Wild Irish Rose

Moderately flowing ♩ = 142

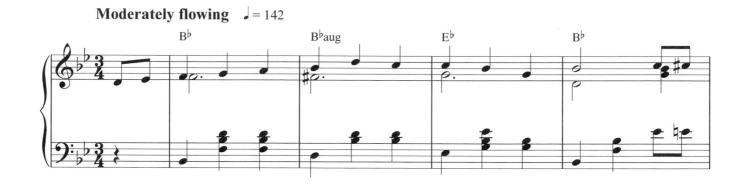

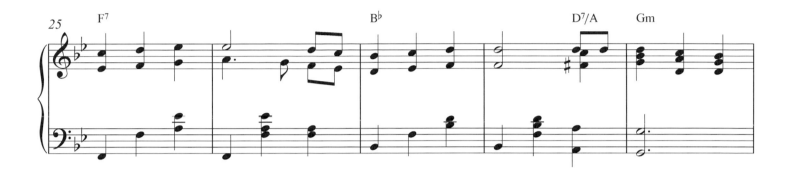

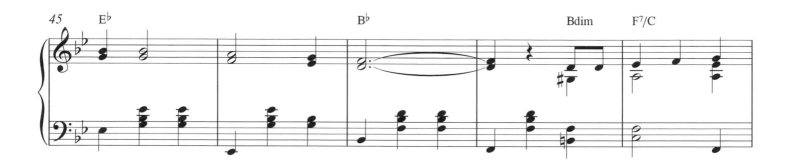

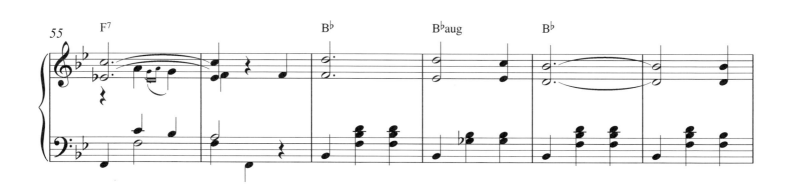

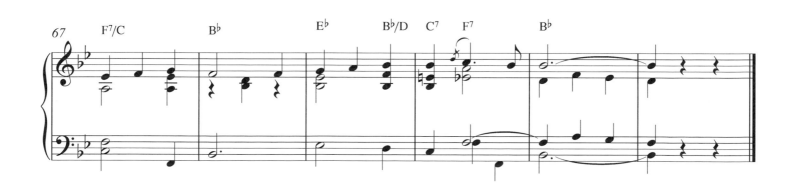

U2
One

Words & Music by David Evans, Adam Clayton, Paul Hewson & Laurence Mullen

Arranged by Barrie Carson Turner

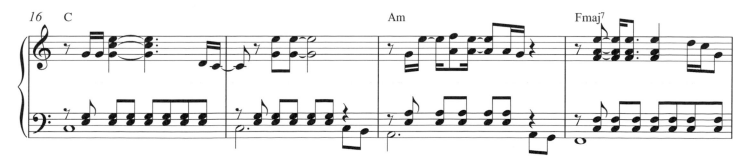

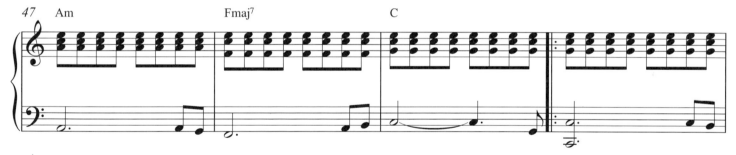

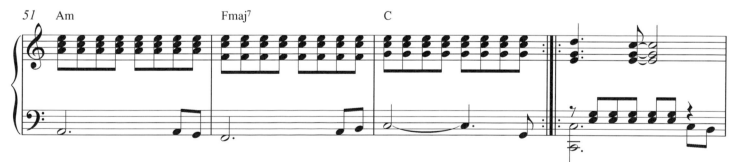

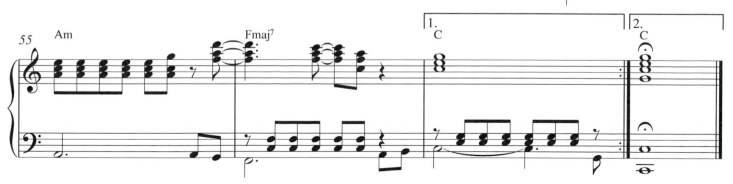

SINÉAD O'CONNOR
Nothing Compares 2 U

Words & Music by Prince

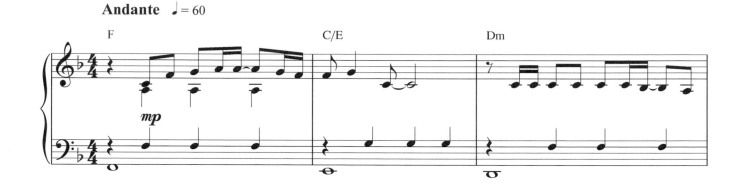

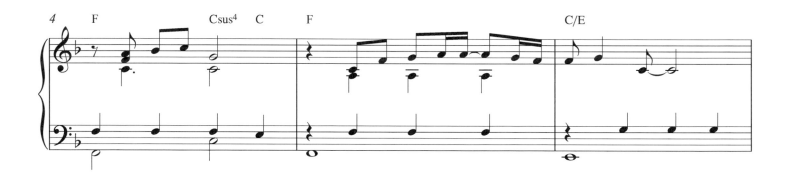

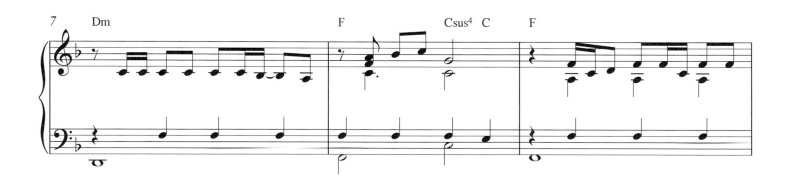

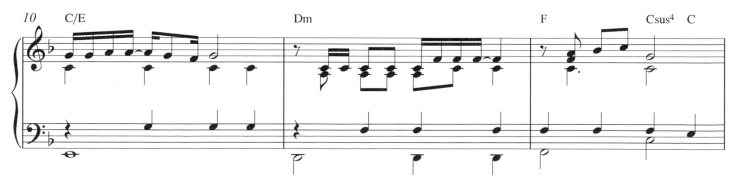

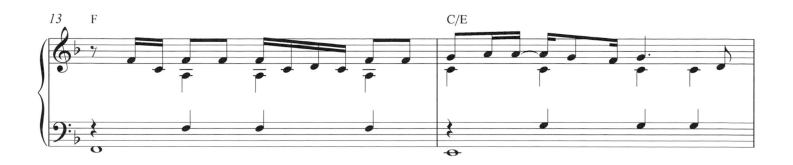

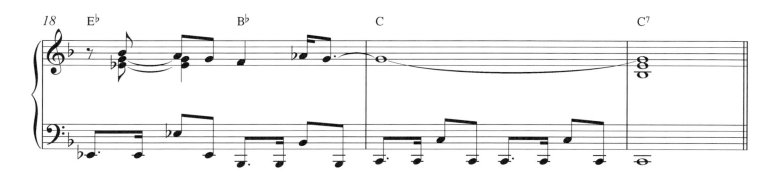

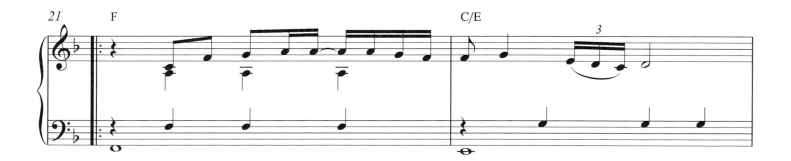

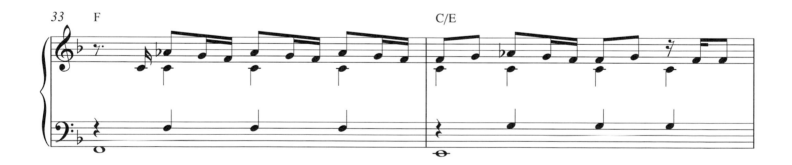

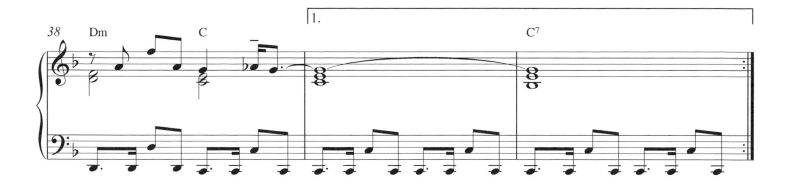

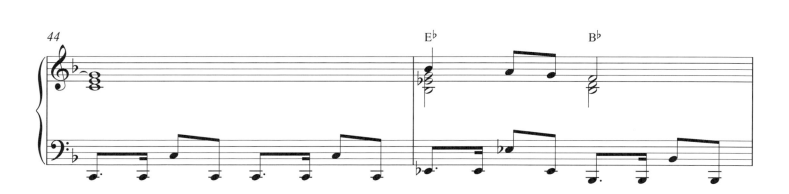

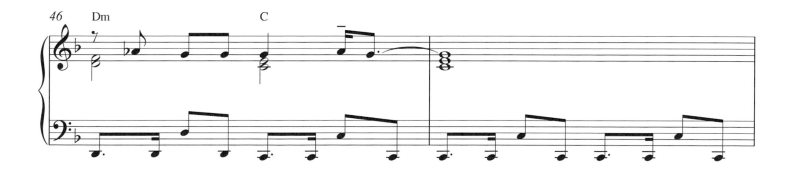

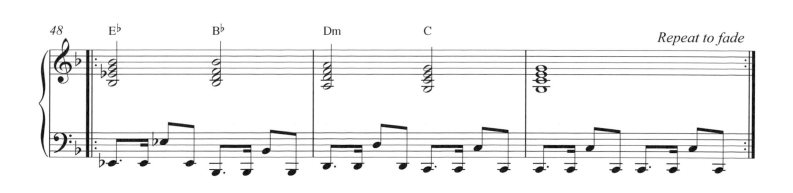

TRADITIONAL IRISH
Rose Of Tralee

Slowly (with feeling) ♩ = 100

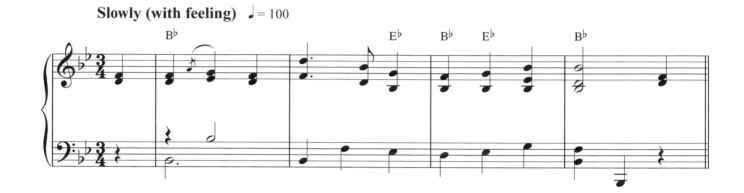

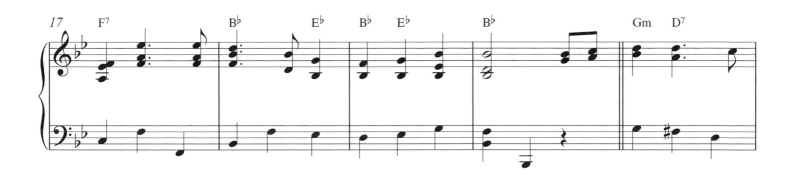

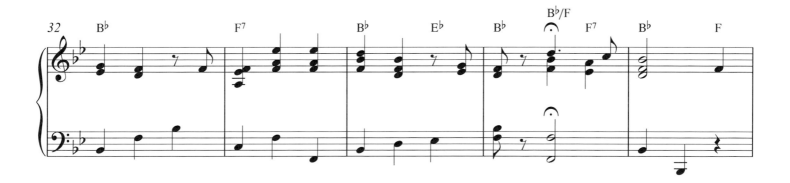

55

THE CORRS
Runaway

Words & Music by Andrea Corr, Caroline Corr, Sharon Corr & Jim Corr

Arranged by Barrie Carson Turner

Moderately ♩. = 50

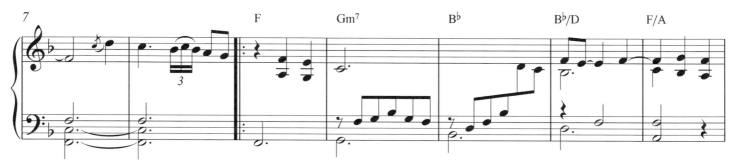

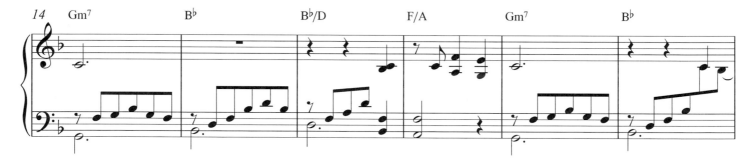

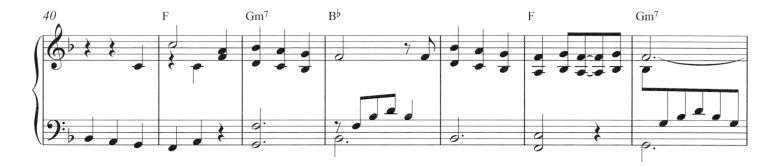

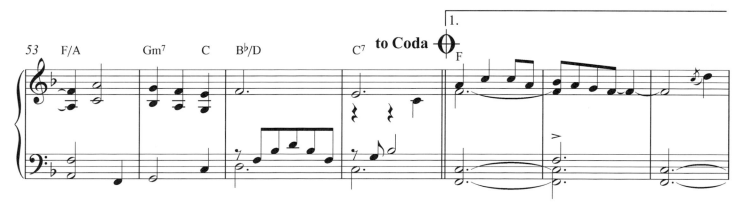

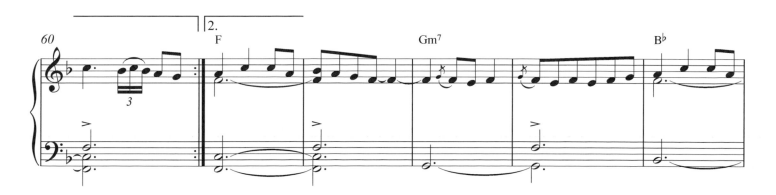

D.S. al Coda

Coda

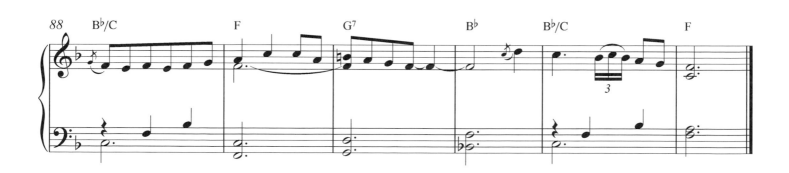

TRADITIONAL IRISH
When Irish Eyes Are Smiling

Words by George Graff & Chauncey Olcott

Music by Ernest Ball

Valse moderato espressivo ♩ = 122

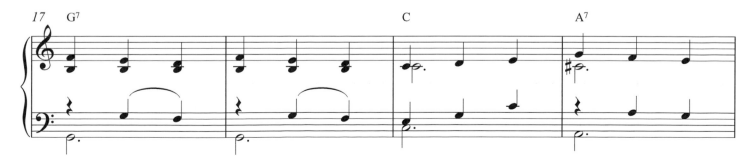

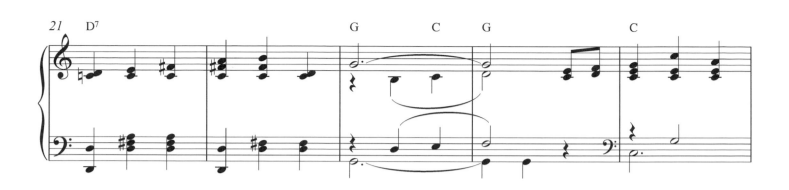

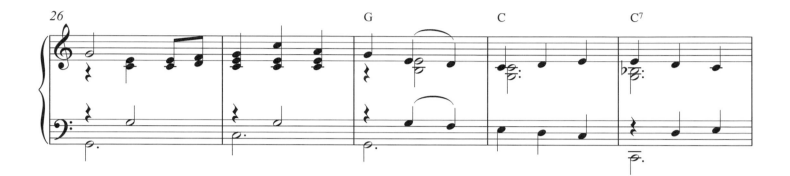

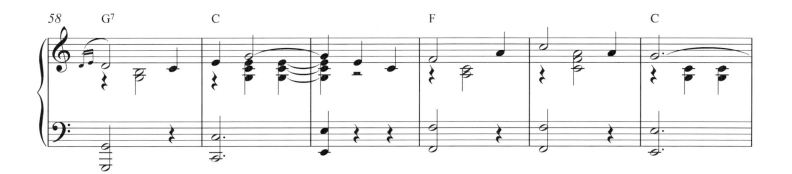

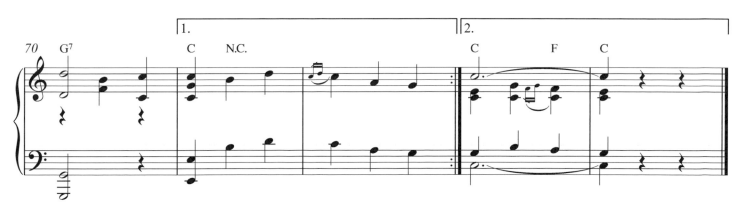

BOYZONE
When You Say Nothing At All

Words & Music by Don Schlitz & Paul Overstreet

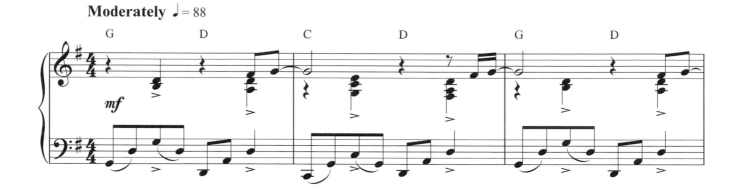

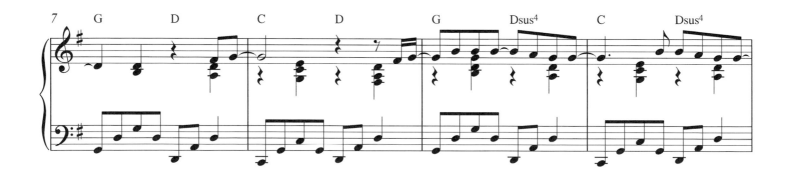

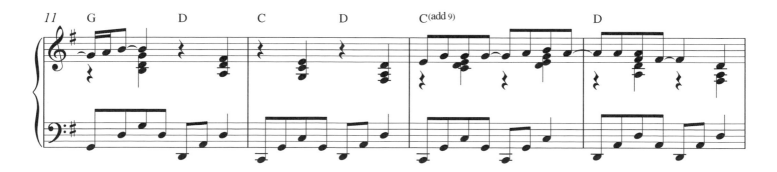

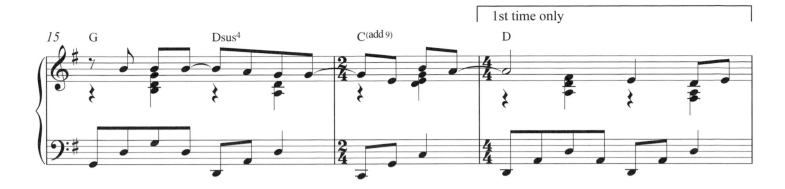

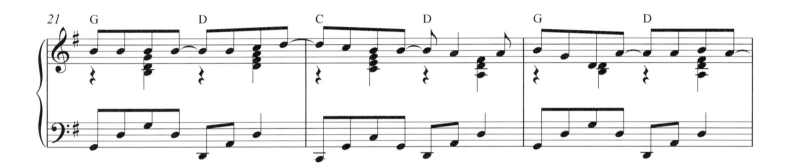

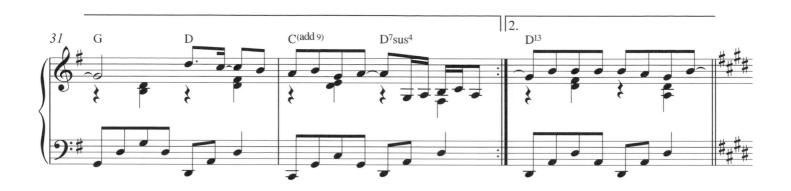

D.S. al Coda   **Coda**

TRADITIONAL SCOTTISH
Auld Lang Syne

Words By Robert Burns

Andante con moto

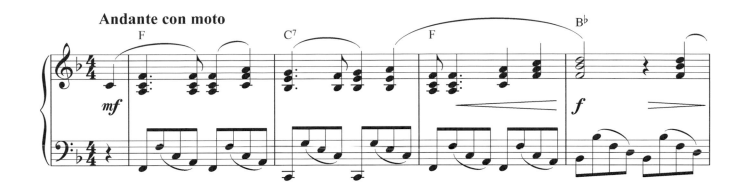

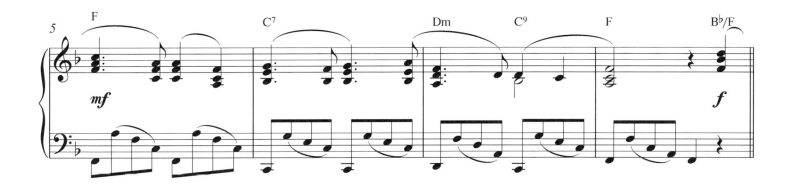

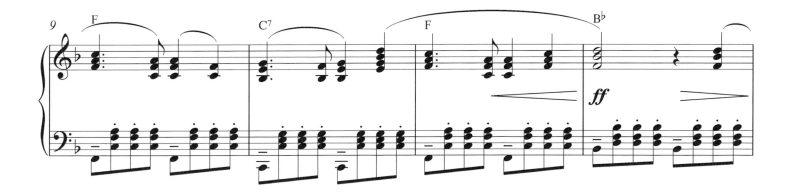

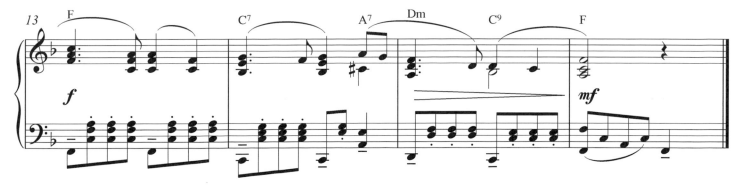

TRADITIONAL SCOTTISH
The Bluebells Of Scotland

Moderately

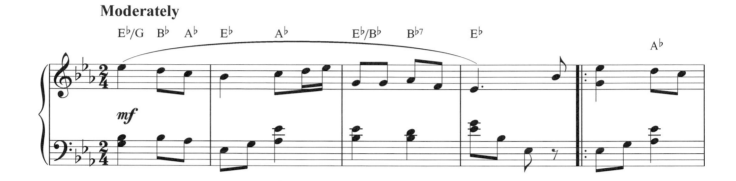

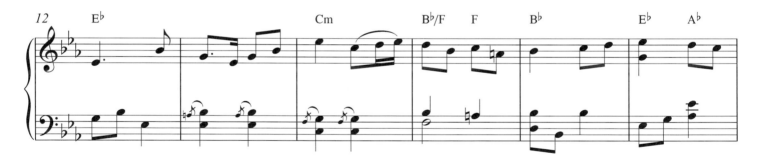

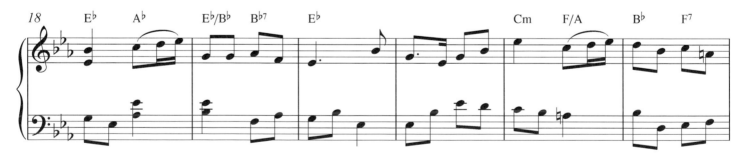

TRADITIONAL SCOTTISH
Loch Lomond

THE PROCLAIMERS
Letter From America

Words and Music by Charles Reid & Craig Reid

Arranged by Martha Kent

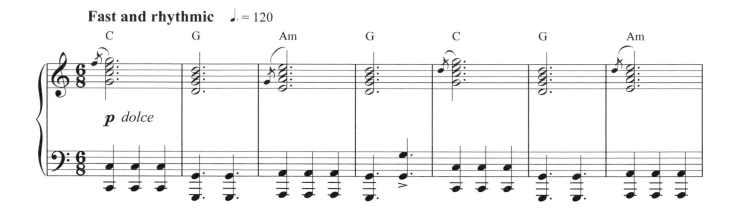

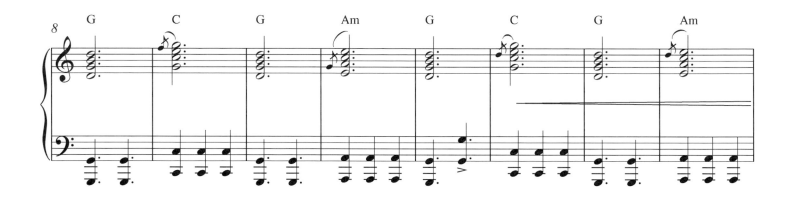

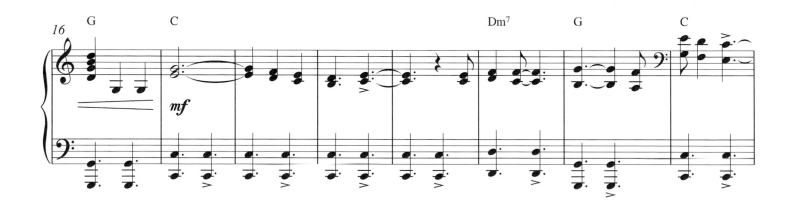

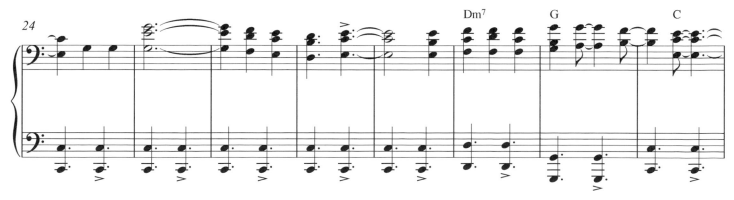

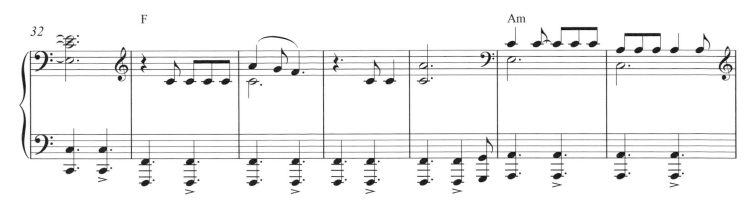

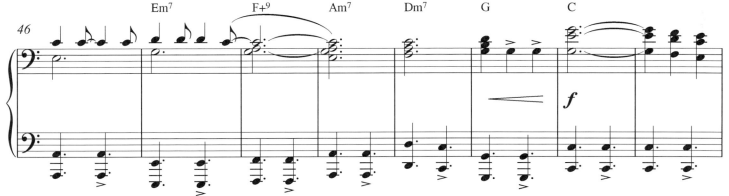

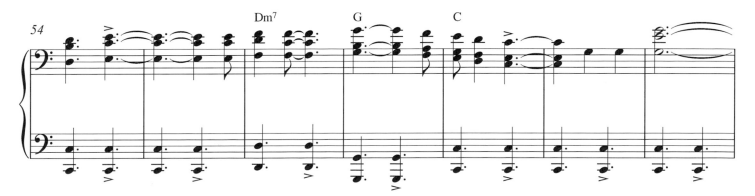

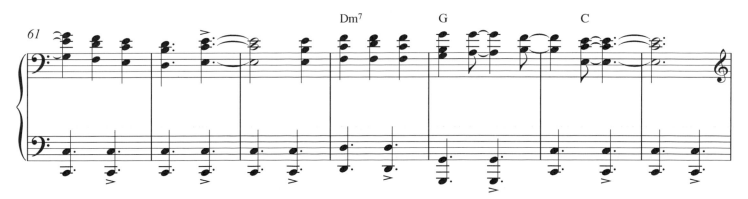

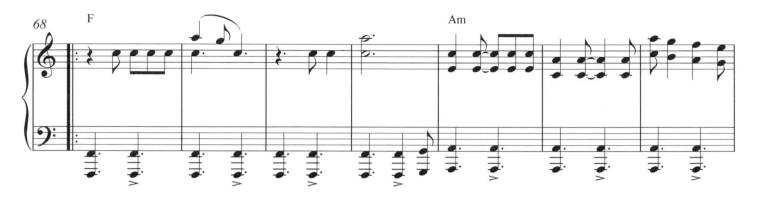

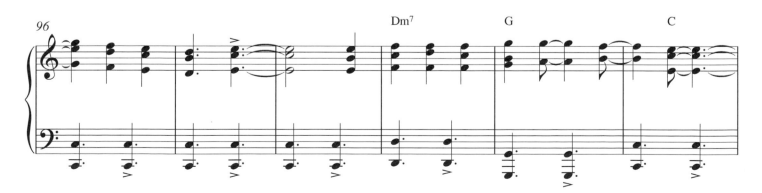

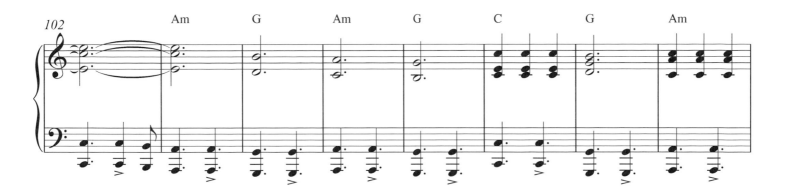

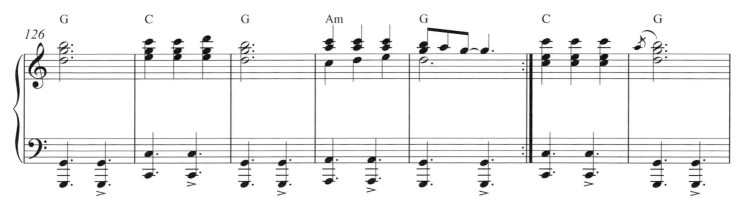

rit.   **Largo**

WET WET WET
Love Is All Around

Words & Music by Reg Presley

Andante ♩ = 85

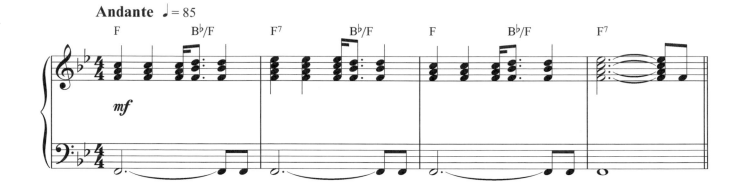

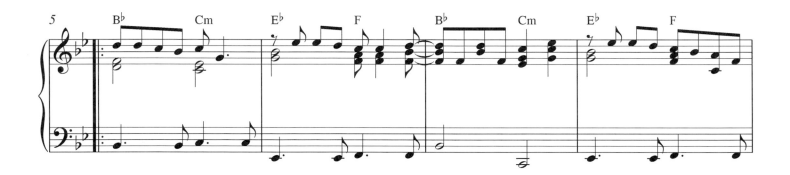

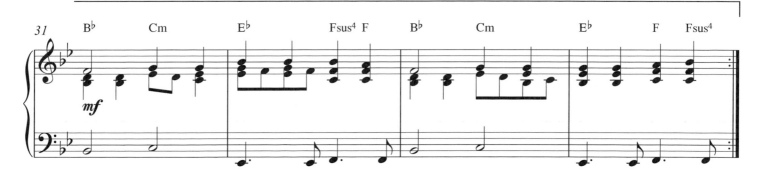

WINGS
Mull Of Kintyre

Words & Music by Paul McCartney & Denny Laine

Slow ♩ = 88

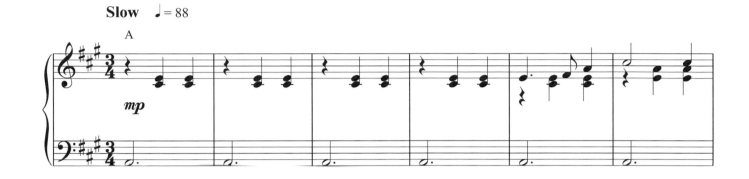

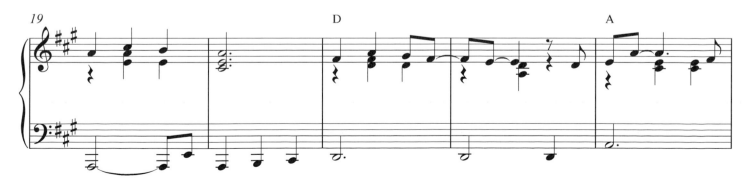

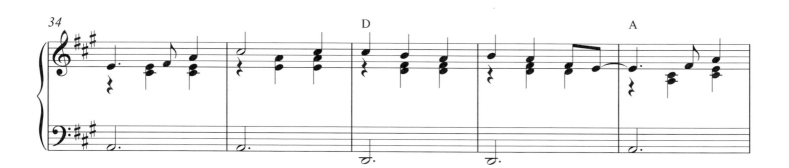

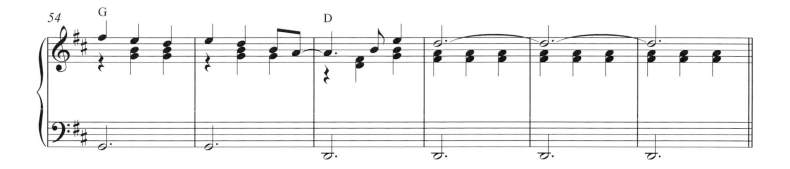

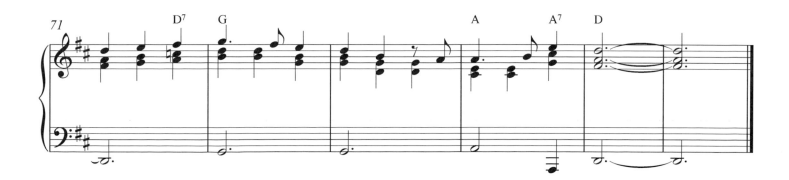

TRADITIONAL SCOTTISH
My Bonnie Lies Over The Ocean

Smoothly

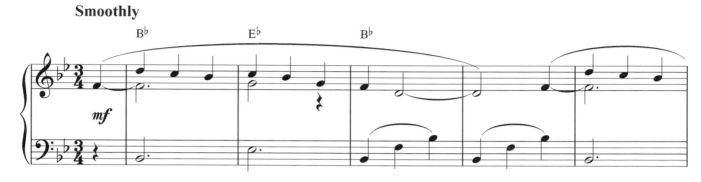

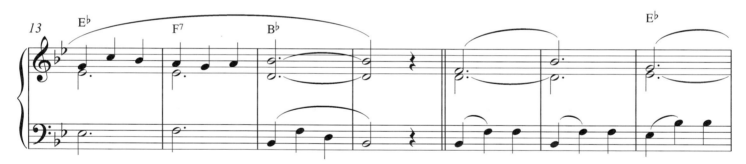

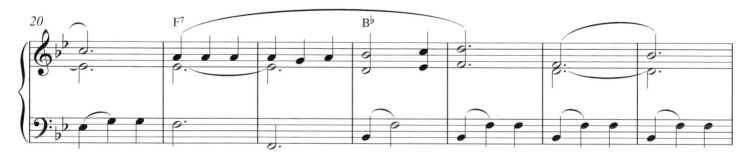

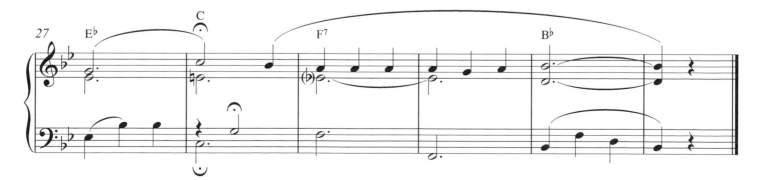

TRADITIONAL SCOTTISH
O, Charlie Is My Darling

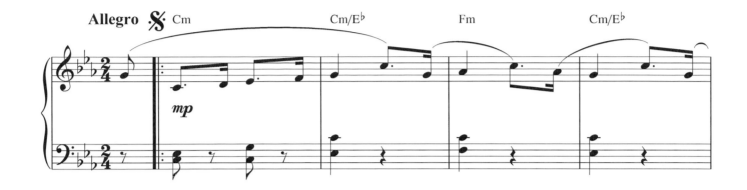

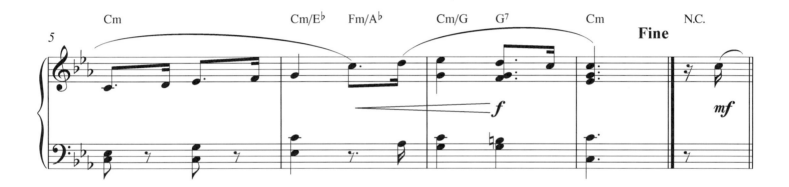

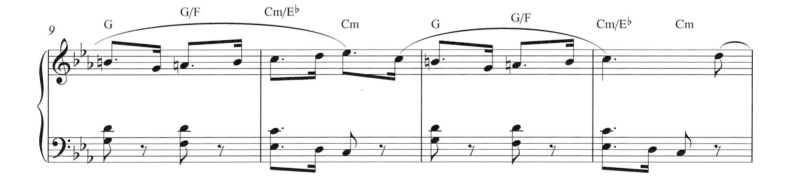

TRADITIONAL SCOTTISH
Skye Boat Song

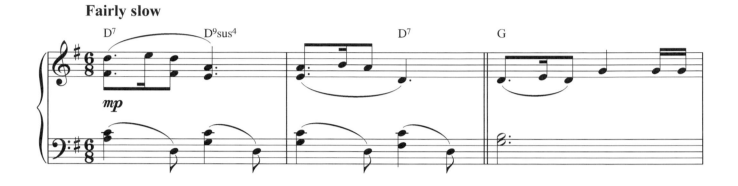

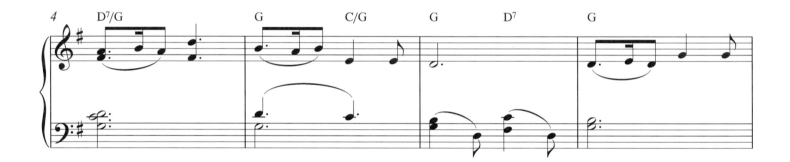

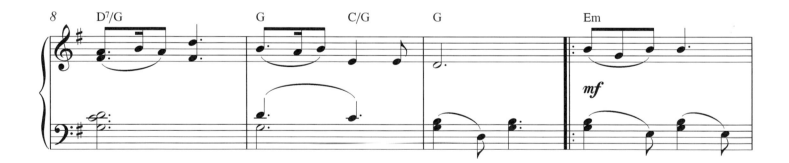

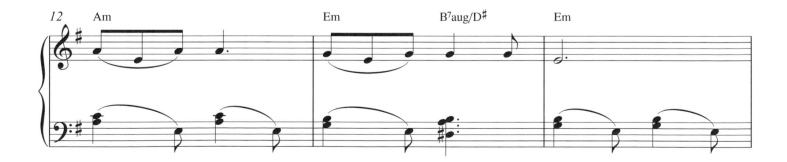

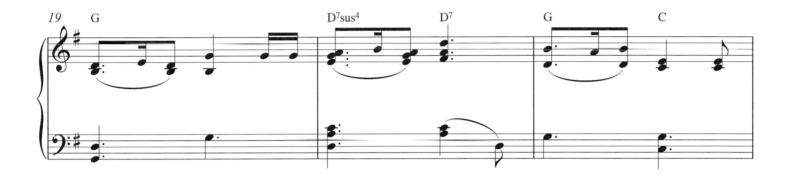

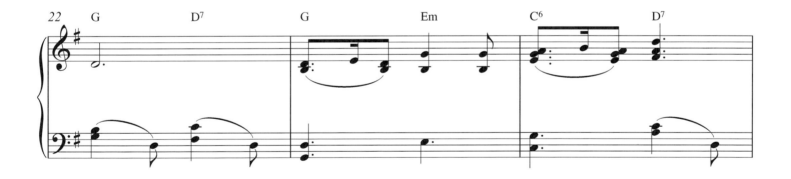

2nd time: rit.

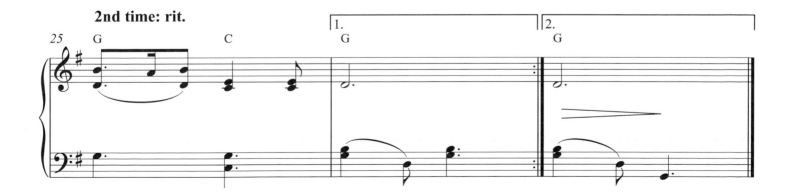

TRADITIONAL WELSH
All Through The Night
(Ar hyd y nos)

Moderato

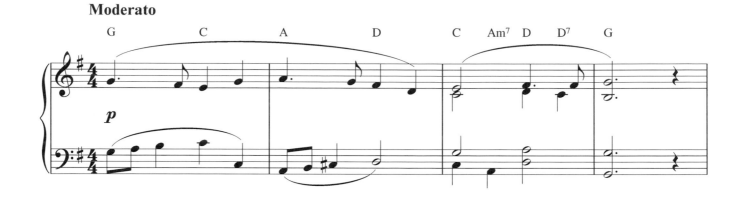

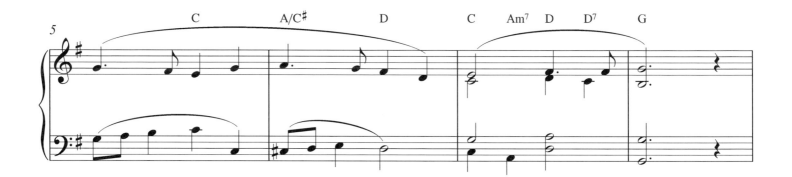

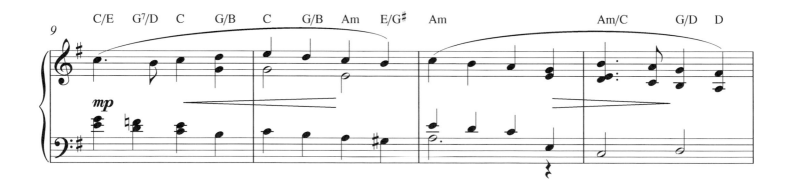

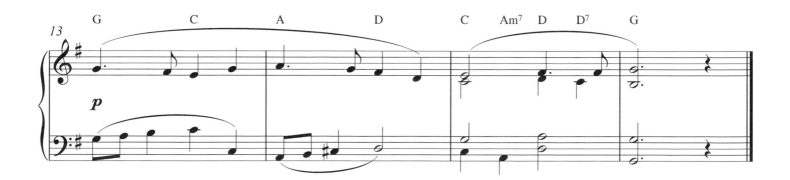

TRADITIONAL WELSH
The Ash Grove

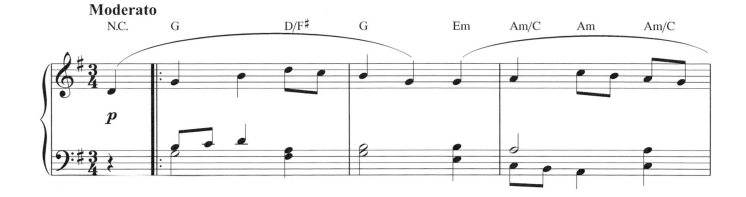

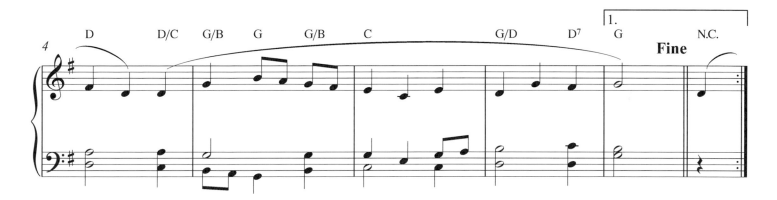

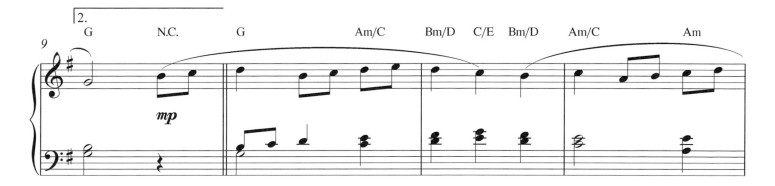

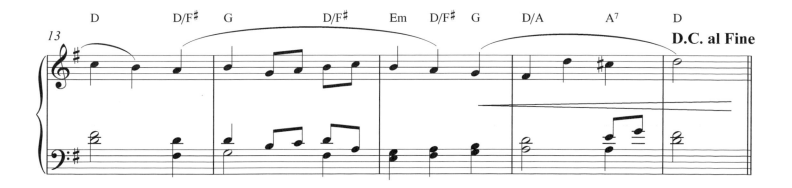

STEREOPHONICS
Have A Nice Day

Words & Music by Kelly Jones

Medium rock ♩ = 120

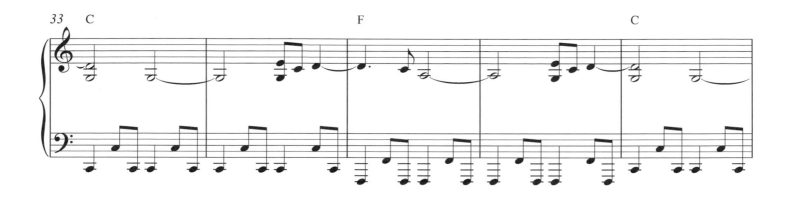

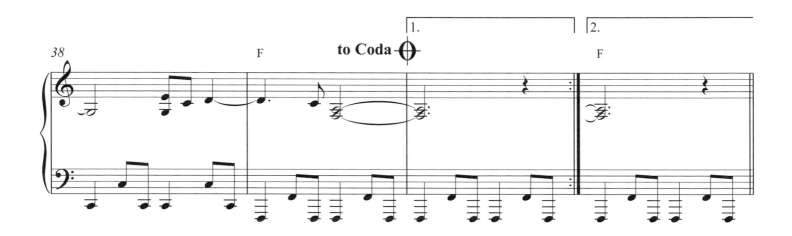

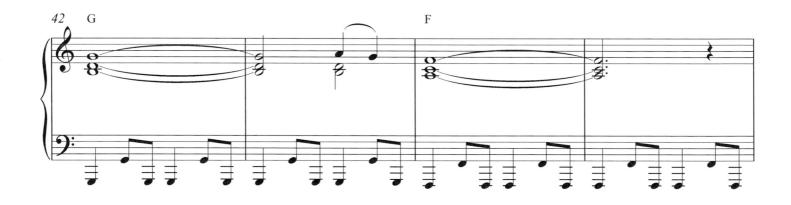

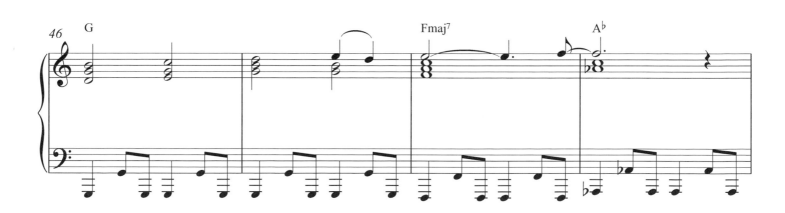

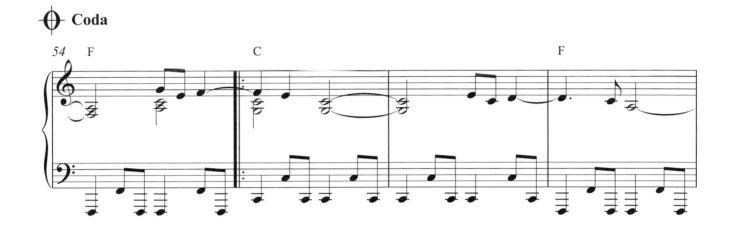

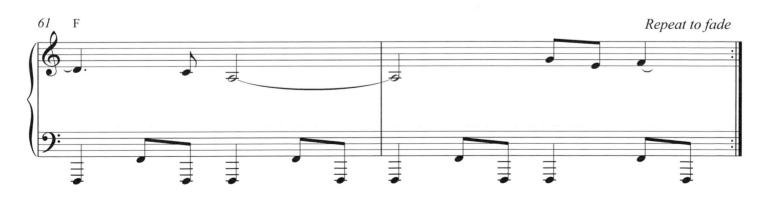

TRADITIONAL WELSH
Men Of Harlech

Alla marcia

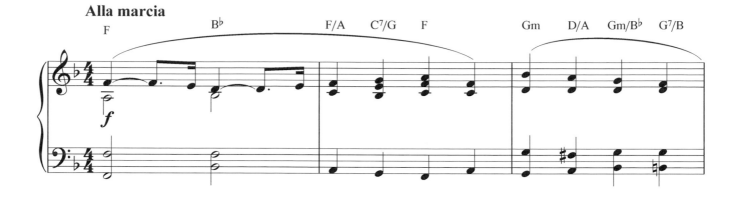

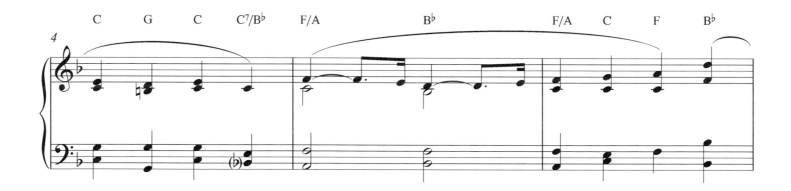

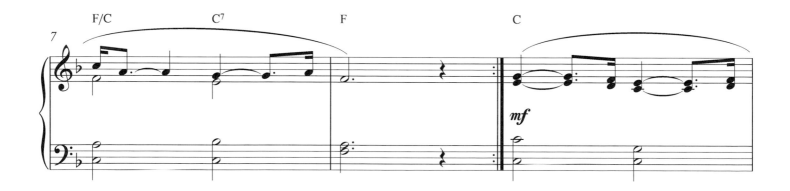

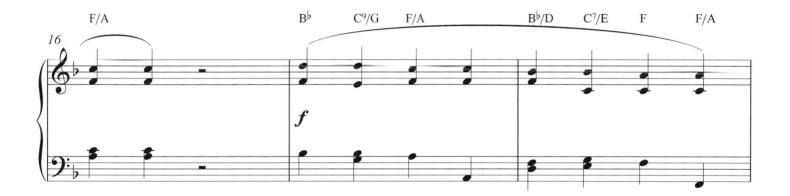

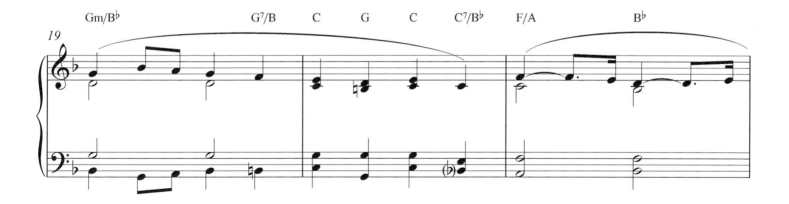

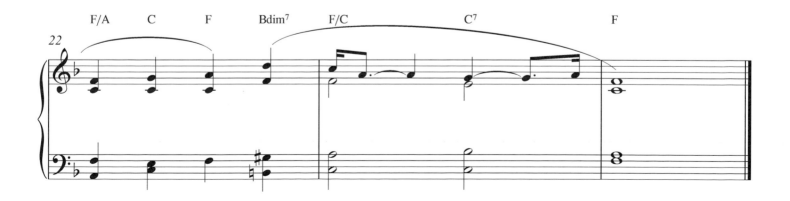

CATATONIA
Road Rage

Words & Music by Cerys Matthews, Mark Roberts, Aled Richards, Paul Jones & Owen Powell

Relaxed ♩ = 96

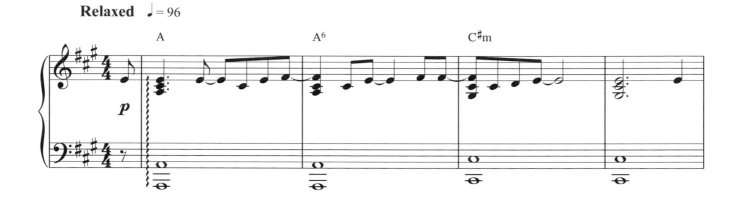

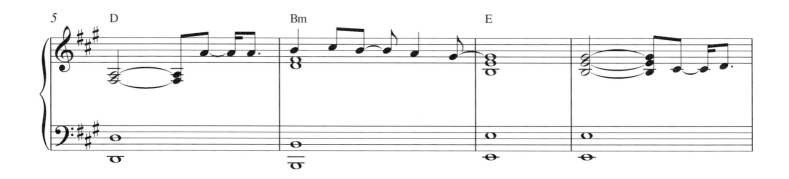

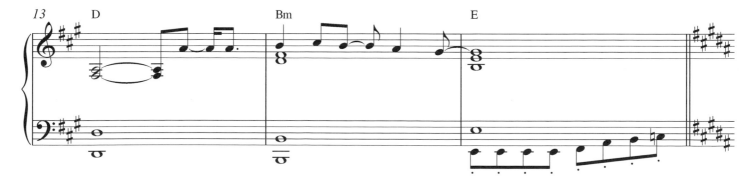

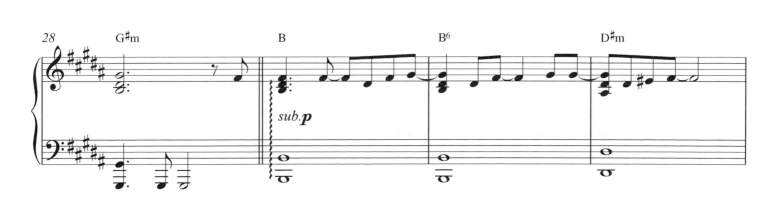

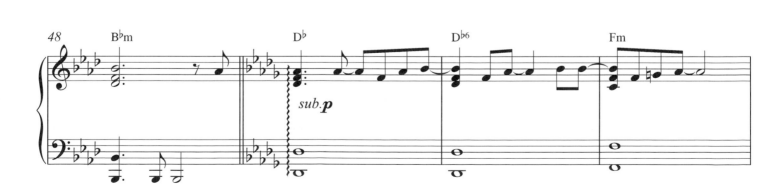

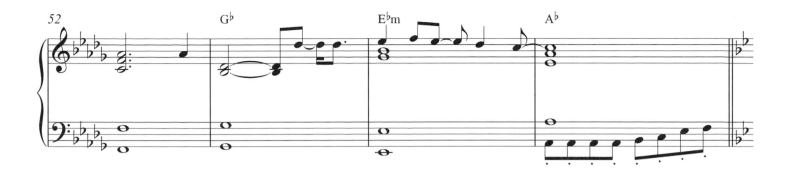

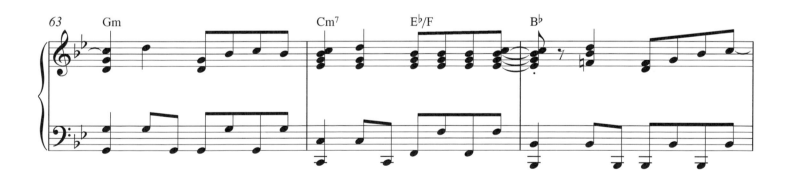

TRADITIONAL WELSH
We'll Keep A Welcome

Words by Lyn Joshua & James Harper and Music by Mai Jones

Arranged by Barrie Carson Turner

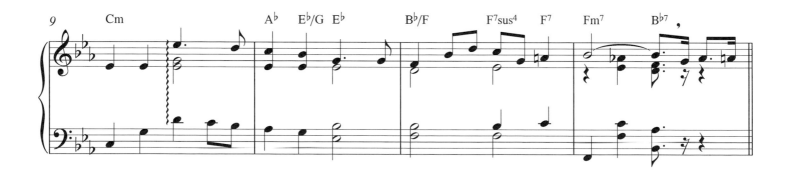

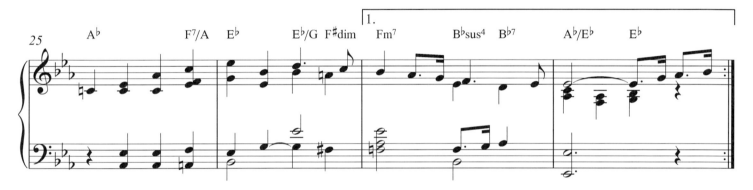

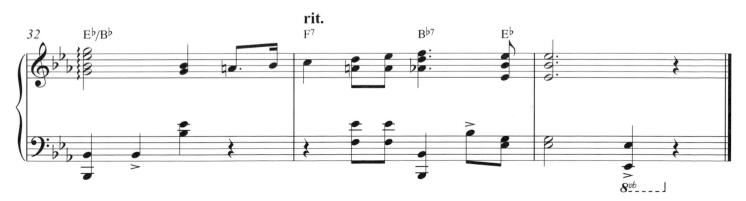

TRADITIONAL WELSH
David Of The White Rock
(Dafydd y Garreg Wen)

Andante

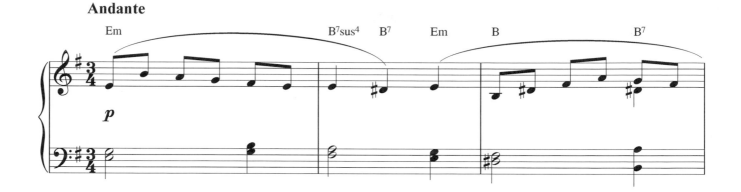

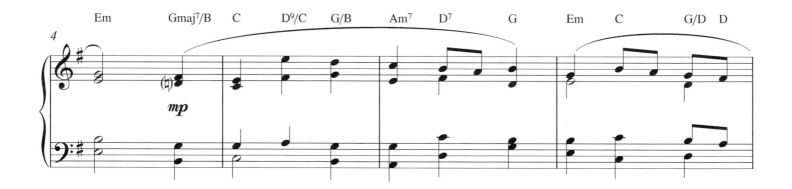

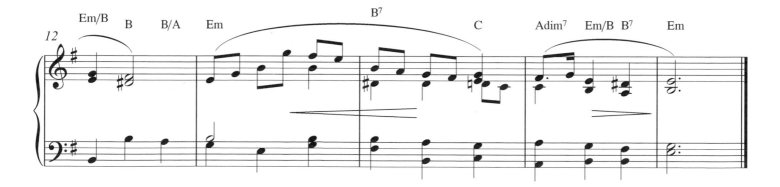